CATNIP

FOR THE

CAT LOVER'S PSYCHE

A Memoir

WITH A FOREWORD BY THE AMAZING KRESKIN

BY

ANN LAPATKA

FULL COLOR EDITION

ISBN: 978-0-578-79177-7

Library of Congress Control Number:
2020921578

Publisher's Cataloging-In-Publication Data
(Prepared by the Donahue Group Inc.)

Names: Lapatka, Ann, author. | Kreskin, 1935- writer of supplementary
    textual content.
Title: Catnip for the cat lover's psyche : a memoir / by Ann Lapatka ;
    [with a foreword by the Amazing Kreskin].
Description: Gouldsboro, Pa. : [Ann Lapatka], [2020]
Identifiers: ISBN 9780578791777
Subjects: LCSH; Lapatka, Ann | Cat owners—Biography. | Cats—anecdotes.
    | Human-animal relationships—Anecdotes. | LCGFT: Autobiographies. |
    Anecdotes.
Classification LCC SF442.82.L36 A3 2020 | DDC 636.80092—dc23

Ann Lapatka
P.O. Box 923
Gouldsboro, PA. 18424

Email: annlapatka777@yahoo.com

Printed in the United States of America

Lapatka Press

DEDICATION

To my three cats:
Toby, Remy, and Mid-night

Their loving Creator,

Rev. Maria D' Andrea
For her wise counsel

and

"The Amazing Kreskin"
for believing in me

You are <u>all</u> "amazing"!

FOREWORD

It is twice that I have read Ann Lapatka's *Catnip for the Cat Lover's Psyche*. It has been a beautiful experience. In writing about the 3 cats in her life, she will be communicating to you, the reader, the feelings and joy that her pets have given her. There is a very good chance that you will read this book not once, but twice, with the likelihood that the second time you'll be sharing it with someone else...just by hearing the words and expressions, they will be entranced with this moving, true story. Today I have 4 cats and through the years it's always been 3 or 4. In the later years of my mother's life, one particular cat became almost an inseparable companion. This book has reawakened in me cherished memories of my pets through the years. You, my dear reader, will realize that cats don't betray people, they add a special joy to our lives, and you're about to experience beautifully expressed hints of that joy.

The Amazing Kreskin

INTRODUCTION

Ann has a unique way of looking at cats, from a rather wonderful sense of humor to making you feel like you are a part of their world.

She brings you into her life and loves, making you feel as though you are family. Her love and understanding of cats is on the spiritual level, and you can't help but being drawn into her thoughts.

Cat lover or not, Ann gives you an insight that will leave you feeling a connection to the feline world.

– Maria D'Andrea MsD, D.D., DRH

TABLE OF CONTENTS

Pawprint of Approval

UPTOWN/DOWNTOWN FELINES

It was pandemonium! Cats, cats, and more cats of all varieties, ranging from the luxurious "Zsa Zsa" types, as I refer to those uptown felines such as Persians and Angoras, sumptuously wrapped in their ridiculously thick fur coats, with soft pink snubby noses and oft blank expressions. Much like, I thought, some humans appear gorgeous on the outward appearance but lack substance. (Well, being a plain human, it's of some comfort).

Then there were the so-called "everyday" ones, such as the Domestic Shorthairs who, again like yours truly, must depend more on their personalities and intelligence to gain approval. (OK, so I have a complex). And then there are those somewhere in between.

CAT-NAPPED!

But they all had one thing in common. These feral cats were all being herded onto a crowded truck barreling toward the Bronx where they would be neutered or spayed, recover consciousness and then, dazed, unceremoniously but safely deposited back onto the mean streets from whence they came. They will never be able to reproduce again after their own kind. There was no way one could, of course, convince them that this was for their own good, but they did not know this now. They were simply petrified and confused, hysterically awaiting their fate from the strange abduction. Similar emotions, I suppose, to humans who claimed they were abducted by UFOs—only now, to these abductee cats, we were the aliens!

"Remy." The cat in an attempted "beaming up"
abduction by a UFO!

When it was finally over they were back to their homeless street life. Things resumed just as before the abduction, only now one could only surmise the psychological repercussions. Did they have PTSD (Post Traumatic Stress Disorder) and flashbacks? And I wondered if they ever had disturbing dreams about their experience. I want to make it clear that I am in no way criticizing those who perform "trap-neuter-return" or TNR services – just attempting to have a "cat-mind" about it. I realize that they have the cats' best interest at heart.

Little did I suspect that out of this debacle some of these felines of the lower echelons of cat society would bless, enrich, and yes – even surprise me – in totally unexpected ways. But at first, I'd like to give a little background of my childhood memories of cats.

"Dustin"

My friend Mary's kitten.

In the beginning...

My earliest recollections of cats were rather insignificant – mostly wild, scruffy strays who wandered by the house, and since we fed them, kept returning for more. It was a superficial relationship of necessity. (Are some humans much better, staying in relationships for material gain?) They usually ran away, mainly due to my constant attempts at picking up and holding them, at which time they would frantically squiggle out of my arms and escape. Then we would get a replacement cat, and this scenario would repeat itself again and again, much to my upset. It makes me call to mind a woman whose cat, she says, was a rude, obnoxious and gluttonous creature who slovenly gulped down his food as soon as it hit the dish, then raced out the door – an ingrate with all the affection of a dead houseplant!

It was my nature, I suppose, to overdo things, such as when I overfed the goldfish in their bowl, only to discover them floating on the water's surface the following day. The cats fared better and were luckier, since they were able to escape my childish ministrations. But it was all out of love! So I grew up not really expecting much satisfying feedback from the cat-human relationship, nor did I have a particularly high regard for the Felidae species.

A rare childhood photo of the author pushing a cherished creature in a doll carriage.

BLUE-EYED, BROWN-EYED CAT

Another incident that for some reason oddly remains etched in my memory after all these years, is that of my childish exuberance in hearing from a very elated and out of breath playmate of a certain cat, down by the Passaic River, who actually had two different colored eyes. WOW! Well this was high adventure, and we ran as fast as we could down to the river to witness this "miracle." And, sure enough, my playmate was right. There was the cat with one brown and one blue eye, placidly reclining on the river bank. He must have wondered what all the excitement was all about, what with us wide-eyed kids peering intently into his eyes, just inches away from his face! The poor creature took it very well. It makes me wonder why a human with two different colored eyes is not received with such enthusiasm, but even ostracized.

Well, you've heard about the cat with "all the affection of a dead houseplant." On the opposite end of the spectrum, it is said, thankfully, that cats do exist whose owners (or from a cat's perspective, equal partners) love and cherish their felines so much that they will change the colors of their wardrobes to match their shedding. It is from this category, I am happy to say, that I have had several "relationship cats," as I call them. I have heard it said that cats got a bad rap due to all the mischief the Siamese cats got into in Disney's *Lady and the Tramp*. I hope my story will help to quell some of these notions. And I am in very good company, as you will read in the next chapter.

WHY I AM A CAT-O-LIC

There's a good chance, if you've been drawn to this book, that you are already a "CAT-O-LIC," but may never have considered yourself as such. Or the realization could have almost imperceptibly begun to dawn on you, as it did to me, that there is "something more" to your little friend, innocently lapping her milk from a saucer, than meets the eye. If you have your intuition is shared with Pharaohs, kings, statesmen, and other dignitaries who greatly revered and admired—even worshipped—these members of the Felidae species as deities.

The Egyptian sun god, Ra, even took the form of a spotted cat. And the Egyptian Maus cats were esteemed as sacred by the ancient Egyptians. The Pharaohs were, of course, most intelligent and spiritually discerning. These cats' "eyeliner" markings were so admired that the Pharaohs even had their eye makeup applied in imitation.

Also, they were honored in the Egyptian culture's preparation for the afterlife. Mummified cats are displayed in the British Museum in London — esteemed so highly that the Pharaohs desired to be buried with them to enjoy their companionship in the afterlife.

CAT MUMMY

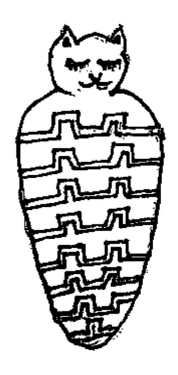

Desirable companion of the Great Pharaohs in the Afterlife.

An Irish legend states:

> *"A cat's eyes are windows enabling*
> *us to see into another world."*

French historian and critic Hippolyte Taine (1828-1893) believed:

> *"I've met many thinkers and many cats, but the*
> *wisdom of cats is infinitely superior."*

The Egyptian Pharaohs knew this.

Dear God, make me worthy of my cat!

Even at this age, the author was pondering

the spirituality of cats.

CATS FOR CANONIZATION

Your little friend, whom you observe toying with her ball of yarn, has virtues already naturally embedded in her that mystics, yogis, and those fasting and praying as they aspire to sainthood have not yet attained. For example, did you know that it took Saint Francis de Sales twenty years to conquer his impatience? I could not help but admire the patience my beloved cat, Remy, displayed when he waited, transfixed for sometimes hours, intensely concentrating at the space underneath the kitchen stove for the poor unfortunate mouse who would eventually stumble in from the cold. When Remy finally and joyfully claimed his prey, there would be no whining about how long it took to achieve success. He promptly forgot about the pain of endurance and proceeded to his next venture. He was already an expert in mindfulness – no lessons necessary, a level I have never been able to achieve.

—ANN LAPATKA

THE FREUDIAN CAT

Indeed, even Sigmund Freud believed that "Time spent with cats is never wasted." He also said: "I prefer the company of animals more than the company of humans." Certainly not what I expected to discover when I researched this world famous psychoanalyst.

Therefore, I could only surmise the subtle mysteries of the psyche transpiring between Freud and his feline "subjects," since he also perceived:

"We choose not randomly each other. We meet only those who already exist in our subconscious."

It is with this in mind that I will attempt to explore the more subtle aspects of the cat-human relationships that I have been privileged to experience in my lifetime. I do this with joy and even more confidence than I had previous to my discovery of these famous lovers of cats. They already existed in my subconscious, and now I will try and put into words what my subconscious has known all along.

The mystery unfolds...

My kitty already existed in my subconscious.

TOBY'S STORY

PAW PRINTS IN THE SNOW

Everything was white. Several inches of snow had softly fallen overnight, pristinely blanketing the small suburban town. Tranquility reigned and all was still – but wait, not all. The movement of something, which perfectly matched the newly fallen snow...a white cat, extremely frail and stick-like, with bones protruding from apparent near-starvation, slowly and laboriously trudged its way through the snow's depth. It was clearly at death's door, there was no doubt about that.

Almost miraculously, this lone stick-figure managed to meander its way to my friend, Mary's house, which already housed several cats in addition to feeding outdoors an increasingly growing population of ferals. This was not looked upon kindly by the neighborhood. A vengeful neighbor even photographed one of Mary's housecats as it peeked out her window. The photo was then given to the township to prove that she had one cat too many in her home – but that is another story in itself.

Here, Toby, as I named him, found compassion— but not from the strays who saw him as competition, as they took turns blocking the path to him at feeding time. Poor Toby! It was survival of the fittest, and they sized up his weakness, taking full advantage of the situation.

Mary was quick to observe this scenario and arranged her busy schedule to accommodate Toby, at a different time, when the strays had gone. He gradually gained weight and strength, flourishing under the care of a sympathetic, elderly veterinarian who accepted very reduced fees to help with Mary's charitable work.

Finding a "pet parent" to adopt Toby was becoming problematic. Mary told me that people were often extremely picky about a cat's appearance and health, which often determined their fate. Not surprisingly, I suppose, humans frequently do likewise with each other, possibly forfeiting what could be a fulfilling relationship. Toby's appearance was rather ordinary — short white hair with some sparse orange markings and a fluffy orange and white striped tail (the tail of which was quite to my liking).

As fate would have it, Mary and I were talking on the phone about my adopting Toby. She told me that we wouldhave to catch him when he crossed her street. Toby was in the habit of doing so every day between 5:00 and 7:00pm for his supper. Mary surmised that he was staying in some abandoned house, but no one knew for sure where he came from.

Well, as we spoke, she suddenly exclaimed that Toby was crossing the street right now! Hastily jumping into my car, I made a beeline to Mary's house, where she trapped Toby in a cage, along with a soft blanket and some food, for transit to my cottage in the country. I placed Toby's cage next to me on the front seat of my car, occasionally sticking my fingers through its bars to pet and soothe him. He softly meowed in apprehension of what awaited him. It seemed like an eternity as I made the two-hour drive home, feeling much sympathy for the little captive beside me.

Toby's Home at last!

THE CATNIP DAYS

Finally we arrived, and I carried the cage into my cottage, carefully closing my front door, so that Toby would not have an opportunity to escape when I opened the cage. Very nervous, Toby furtively glanced about his new strange surroundings, then speedily darted into a space behind the kitchen cabinets. He remained there as long as I was awake. The food and water I left out overnight were consumed when I awoke in the morning. My phantom kitty repeated this pattern for several days before he felt trusting enough to make his appearance, (I had heard of a neighbor's cat who took two weeks to come out, so I didn't consider this too bad.)

Since Toby had been a feral cat living outdoors, being in the house all the time did not suit him in the least. He was clearly frustrated and longing for the outdoor stimulation he had once enjoyed. It was only a matter of time before someone left the door ajar and Toby escaped. He knew the inside of my cottage but was not acclimated to my yard, so he would not be able to recognize my home from the outside in case he was lost. After some attempts to find him, I frantically phoned Mary, when suddenly Toby casually strolled through the open door. I had a red heart-shaped tag with my phone number engraved on it made, but he was never "lost" again. I think the little stinker knew exactly what he was doing. I recommend acclimating your pet to the outdoors, so he can become familiar with it, even if he is kept as an indoor pet.

So from this time on, Toby lived out what I called the "Catnip Days" — something parallel to what humans would experience in their "Days of Wine and Roses!" It gave me such joy to watch him eat his "Fancy Feast" cat food with gusto. From time to time he'd pensively tilt his head to the side while chewing his gourmet food, and I imagined he might have been pondering how he had suffered privation in the past and how his luck had now turned for the best. Toby was home!

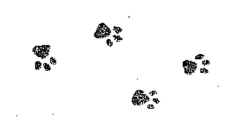

TOBY DBA "LITTLE LOVER"

It didn't take long for Toby and I to bond. We had something in common and that was, sorry to say, suffering. A true companion pet, most empathetic and uncannily perceptive, his furry paw had "just the right touch" when he patted me as I was sad or going through problems. Toby just "knew." And his feline spirit radiated an energetic but soothing aura which pervaded my tiny A-frame cottage, playing no small part in making a house a home.

"I love cats because I enjoy my home, and little by little, they become its visible soul."

-Jean Cocteau

When asked why I am not married, the answer is simple: The males whose qualities I covet are either all in monasteries – or they are CATS!

As Brigitte Bardot comments:

"I really am a cat transformed into a woman."

And Charles Dickens ponders:

"What greater gift than the love of a cat?"

A CAT'S PRIDE

Since I had to be away frequently for work, naturally it was necessary to leave Toby at home, which he deeply resented. When I would return he was clearly miffed and would turn away from me. I perceived that his feelings were not only hurt, but also his pride (remember, he's a male). He thought about how I could dare leave him and then return, expecting our relationship to resume just as it had before. The nerve! I felt very bad, but of course I could not explain to him, that if he wanted his "Fancy Feast" gourmet cat food, I had to go out and earn the money. But after a short interval he would cave in to my attempts to "reconcile" (especially after a tasty treat).

Lest one may think I have an overactive imagination in this matter, I am in good company. The famous author, poet, and critic, Edgar Allan Poe, experienced something similar. His very sensitive black cat, Catterina, suffered intense anxiety from Poe's comings and goings, even refusing to eat until he came back. When he was writing, she would keep him company, purring as she sat on his shoulders.

"If you want to write, keep cats."
-Aldous Huxley (1894-1963)

I can only hope that yours truly would have similar success in my writing, since my black cat, Mid-night, lies next to me as I author this book. (Well, at least she thinks I'm a success!)

ANNIE THE "HUNTER"

Once upon returning home I brought a can of Toby's favorite "Fancy Feast." A friend told me that he felt intuitively that in his cat mind Toby believed that I had returned from hunting to give him this prey (never mind that it came in a can). So I think it's a good idea when you come back from a trip to immediately give your cat a treat. If he thinks you went hunting for him, you just might be forgiven. I learned my lesson the hard way:

> *I'm only a cat,*
> *And we'll get along fine,*
> *As long as you know*
> *I'm not yours - you're all mine!*
>   —Author Unknown

TOBY "TID-BITS"

As I reclined on the sofa downstairs to watch TV, Toby would keep a watchful eye on me for hours, as he sat on the step of the spiral staircase above. (See photo) It was his favorite spot in the house, next to sleeping with me in bed. Eerily, years after Toby's demise, when I adopted another cat named Remy who tried to sit on or near Toby's spot on the staircase, he acted as if there was something there and kept circling the area, until finally he sat on a different step. I believe it was Toby's ghost still sitting there, watching over me, and that was why Remy did not take Toby's spot.

"TOBY"

Keeping a watchful eye on the staircase.

Although Toby was an excellent mouse-catcher, earning his keep as a member of the household, he strangely befriended a certain chipmunk with whom he cavorted a number of times. He could have easily overcome the miniscule creature but chose instead to befriend it. The two spent happy times playfully jumping and dodging each other on a rock in my yard. It was really a sight to behold. I would not even consider telling this to a veterinarian – he would never believe me.

I recall something I saw once on TV, where a bird actually kept a kitten from starving by feeding it worms, and it was on video. Otherwise no one would have believed it. I've heard of other incidences which are also considered against nature.

Toby enjoyed his look-out post—a huge boulder on my property where he would survey all the action going on in the forest. One encounter which Toby must have regretted was his choice to actually challenge a deer—much larger than himself. The deer charged him and Toby ran into a small space. From then on Toby would hide behind the lattice fence when finally the deer came, nervously and cautiously observing it as it walked in the woods. Perhaps Toby thought the deer didn't belong on his territory, since it came so close to my house. But to challenge an animal so much larger than himself –

Toby, what were you thinking???

Toby keeping a watch over the homestead.

"Hide n' Seek" was another pastime of Toby's. I'd pretend not to see him hiding in the tall grass and kept calling his name. Meanwhile, he'd crouch even lower as I passed by. My friend and I repeatedly asked, "Where's Toby?" as we walked around, and the little stinker reveled in his "secret" hiding place. Finally, there was much excitement on both ends when we "found" Toby who, I suppose, was satisfied that he had fooled us at least for some time.

Toby hiding in the grass.

Like Lassie, Toby exhibited some dog-like behavior. He would break into a run when I called him, which is very unusual for a cat. Of course, this was only when he was in the mood! But I have never known of any other cat who did this. Another thing my veterinarian would never believe.

At other times Toby could be very dignified, jauntily prancing about almost like a miniature white Arabian horse. It was poetry in motion. Again, I have never seen anything quite like it in a cat. Toby had come a long way from that lone stick-figure trudging in the snow.

Lookin' for adventure and whatever comes my way!

There were times that Toby was most displeased with me, like the time I tore apart my bedroom to reorganize. He entered my room, glancing around at the disarray with a look of utter astonishment, which turned to disgust as he stalked out of the room tail up. I had some nerve! After all, he couldn't lie on my bed, which was covered with papers. With a face covered in fur, I find it interesting how one could tell he was disgusted, but he was. Never again, Toby, will you be inconvenienced this way, I promise!

Another incident was when I speedily swung into my driveway with the car. Apparently, Toby had been lying in the middle of the driveway resting, and I had startled him as he ran away just in time. I realized what had happened when his eyes glared, laser-like, and seemingly bore into me most reproachfully. Although he could not speak, I really felt like I had a good scolding for being so careless.

From that time on I was extremely careful when I drove into my driveway. Thank God a tragedy was averted!

EXTRAVAGANT CAMPING

Butterflies and moths fascinated Toby, and it was so comical to watch him as he leaped and tried to swat them with his paws. He helped me see my humble surroundings with a new, fresh perspective. My tiny A-frame cottage was now "extravagant camping," as someone coined the phrase. My woods teemed with abundant life of all kinds, both plant and animal. That is the way Toby viewed his new surroundings, and I began to see things Toby's way.

"Toby" in deep woods.

A MEOW IN TIME

I had purchased a clock which had twelve different breeds of cats painted on it – one cat for each hour. As each hour struck a different breed would meow. Toby would then look around the house for the cat. It was quite humorous to watch him as he searched behind the kitchen cabinets and other nooks and crannies for the cats. Eventually he caught on and ignored the cat's meows, but it was fun while it lasted!

"SOUL CAT"

My most unforgettable experience with Toby was on an incredibly lovely day in all nature's glory. Toby was soaking it all in, as he glanced approvingly in different directions, sizing up his situation and being most pleased. Then he literally beamed with an ethereal glow which startled me and a friend who was with me....it was as if he had seen the Beatific Vision. I am glad I had a witness with me, with whom I speak of this unforgettable experience every now and then, even years after Toby's death. Believe what you will, but you will never convince me otherwise. I know Toby had a soul!

In my opinion, no one does a better job of expanding on this than Wallace Sife, Ph.D. in chapter 16, "Religion and the Death of Pets," of his book *The Loss of a Pet*.

Wallace Sife says that, since we know that animals have a capacity to love, one may wonder if they could possess some spirituality unknown to us.

I highly recommend this book to anyone who loves animals. I cannot speak of it highly enough. It has been a great comfort to me in the grieving process when my own cats passed away.

"I believe cats to be spirits come to earth."

-Jules Verne

"Cats are a mysterious kind of folk. There is more passing in their minds than we are aware of."

-Sir Walter Scott

"Sometimes he will sit on the carpet in front of you looking at you with eyes so melting, so caressing and so human, that they almost frighten you, for it is impossible to believe that a soul is not there."

-Theophile Gautier (1811-1878)

Toby in "Samadhi" (Superconsciousness).

THREE-LEGGED TOBY

Toby had been joyously living out his "Catnip Days" for over three years, when suddenly tragedy struck and another chapter of his life was about to unfold. I had been very strict in enforcing a curfew, since my cat-rescuer friend, Mary, had advised me to bring Toby indoors for the night and early morning hours when the more aggressive animals were about. However, unknown to me as I slept, a friend staying overnight let him out. Soon Toby's cries were heard, along with noise of a scuffle. I ran outside calling his name and he weakly limped up the stairs of my deck, injured and bleeding. Frantically scooping him up in my arms, I rushed him to the veterinarian.

I did not realize the extent of Toby's injuries-they were much more serious than I thought. His little toe had to be amputated, and the bite marks were so deep that it was uncertain whether his left rear leg would have to be amputated. The vet prescribed medication for a period of time and instructed me to bring Toby back, hoping that perhaps his leg might be saved after all. He also said that he was unable to tell what type of animal had attacked Toby. But whatever it was would not let go. Mercifully, I had gotten pet insurance just four months previously which covered almost all of Toby's expenses. This was a great consolation to me, as I never could have paid for all of it. Upon bringing Toby back to the vet after the prescribed medication, it was sadly determined that it was necessary to amputate Toby's leg. I agonized over what was the best for my precious friend. Putting him to sleep was another option. But euthanasia was unthinkable in Toby's case-I just <u>knew</u> Toby would choose to live with three legs. The vet kindly assured me that there were many three-legged cats who lived wonderful lives. As it turned out, the vet's judgment was right. Toby's operation was a success, and he adapted so well that I had to chase him just to keep up! His spirit and resilience was simply amazing, so I figured that if Toby was happy–and he was the one who lost a leg, not I – then why couldn't I be the same?

"Toby"

The "Good Life" at last!

"Toby"

Always faithfully watching...

A SIGN OF A BETTER LIFE

I had asked God for a sign about Toby after his unfortunate encounter with the aggressive animal. Then one night after putting some dry cat food in his dish, I left Toby to eat. Upon returning, the dry morsels of cat food had formed a perfect smile right in the middle of the dish! Amazed, I called my friend, who was most surprised as well. Did an angel come to form the perfect smile in Toby's dish? It seemed to be the answer I had been seeking. However, I soon found that this sign was not to be interpreted in the way I had hoped for, but at least, for Toby it signified that he was soon to gain entrance into a much better world.

Soon after his successful operation another health issue erupted. Toby began throwing up and was gasping for air. Upon being X-rayed, it was discovered that Toby had a huge tumor, and this time it was inoperable. He could not eat or breathe without difficulty. The vet kindly counseled me that it was time to face reality and to consider having Toby euthanized. After all Toby had been through and survived – and now this! He had been so brave. My grief was inconsolable.

After the vet gave me some time alone with Toby to think, I knew that I had to do what was best for my precious, loyal companion. In a room painted sky blue with fluffy white clouds I spent my final moments with Toby, speaking softly to him and stroking his soft white fur. Then when I felt ready to release him into the spirit world, I called for the vet who administered euthanasia. I watched as Toby passed into a better place, where there would be no more suffering.

Shaken, I got into my car and drove home, the empty cage beside me. I wondered if Toby's little spirit was with me in the car, since I thought that he may have not made his transition yet into that beautiful heavenly place that God has prepared for his creatures. The cottage felt strangely vacant, his sweet presence no longer there.

I chose to have Toby cremated, and knew that I would have to return in a week to pick up his cremains. I pondered how I would feel when I did—I did not look forward to it, but I wanted to keep his cremains with me at home, not in some faraway pet cemetery where I could rarely visit. The nearest one was several hours away.

TOBY COMES BACK!

AFTER-DEATH EXPERIENCES

One night I had a dream of Toby sitting on a beautiful carpeted staircase in a mansion. He had a look of puzzlement on his little face, wondering what had happened to him. Yet, he seemed peaceful. I believe he was in transition to a higher realm.

At another time I was holding the beautifully carved wooden box containing his ashes on my lap and crying. I fell asleep on the sofa, when suddenly I heard a loud cat cry. I lowered my arms to the side of the couch and felt that familiar soft fur-it was Toby! I kept stroking him, and then Toby leaped onto my chest and began kneading me over and over with his little white paws. Words are impossible to describe the joy we shared. To my amazement, it was absolutely tangible, not just some smoky vapor.

On another occasion, I was lying on the couch, when there was a sudden tug on the sleeve of my bathrobe! I felt Toby's unique presence – his personality is very distinct. As a friend sat with me on my couch, an apparition of a white cat jumped by my shopping bag, which then fell on the floor. There was no way that the bag would just suddenly fall over by itself.

So these are the after-death experiences I had with my dear Toby. I believe his spirit still comes to visit me. He sits on the spiral staircase overlooking my living room, keeping watch over me. Love transcended two worlds.

I look forward to greeting Toby someday on the other side of the "Rainbow Bridge." I am including a copy of the beautiful poem which was painted on the wall of the veterinarian's office where I said my final good-byes to my dear, loyal forever friend.

RAINBOW BRIDGE

Just this side of Heaven is a place called Rainbow Bridge.
When an animal dies that has been especially close to someone
Here, that pet goes to Rainbow Bridge.
There are meadows and hills for all of our special friends
So they can run and play together.
There is plenty of food, water, and sunshine and our friends
are warm and comfortable.
All the animals that had been ill and old are restored to health
And vigor; those who were hurt or maimed are made whole
And strong again, just as we remember them in our dreams
Of days and times gone by.
The animals are happy and content, except for one small thing;
They miss someone very special, someone who was left behind.
They all run and play together, but the day comes when one
Suddenly stops and looks into the distance.
His bright eyes are intent; his eager body begins to quiver,
Suddenly, he begins to run from the group flying over the green
Grass, his legs carrying him faster and faster.
You have been spotted, and when you and your special friend
Finally meet, you cling together in joyous reunion, never
To be parted again.
The happy kisses rain upon your face; your hands again
Caress the beloved head and you look once more into those
Trusting eyes of your pet, so long gone from your life, but never
Absent from your heart…
Then you cross the Rainbow Bridge together…
Author Unknown…

THE AFTERMATH

Toby's unexpected death had left a deep hole in my heart that seemed impossible to fill. A friend suggested I get an immediate substitute pet the very next day. I was shocked at this seeming insensitivity, but realized that it was well-intentioned. Wallace Sife's counsel in the chapter "Another Pet?" of his book *The Loss of a Pet* aided tremendously in working through my grief and not rushing into another pet relationship before I felt ready. Just as with any other dear friend who died, I needed proper time to mourn my loss. Also, I thought it disrespectful to Toby's memory to not allow a reasonable period of time to pass before I could even consider having another "fur-friend."

I guess I must have had "white cat" imprinted on my subconscious, because I was simply obsessed with having only another Toby, and only a white cat would do. This obsession was, of course, unhealthy, as well as being unfair to compare another cat with (the magnificent!) Toby. The new cat would have its own unique personality, and our relationship would be a different one in its own way. Each cat should be accepted on his own merits. After some months, thankfully, my pain eased somewhat, and I began to be open to other possibilities – and I'm so glad I was!

LOVE IN ANOTHER COLOR

My cat-rescuer friend, Mary, related to me how she had been outside feeding feral cats one bitterly cold Christmas Eve. One cat in particular attracted her attention. Sitting in the center of a freezing Market Street sidewalk, the orange and white domestic shorthair cat suddenly turned its head around and just looked at Mary listlessly. Mary's impression was that he seemed so depressed that he didn't care if he lived or died. She could not resist trapping him and bringing him to a warm, safe environment. Mary later told me that she had dealt with over a hundred cats. This one was the most depressed cat she had ever come across.

As I mentioned previously, Mary told me that people were extremely fussy about a cat's appearance when it came to adoption. As she ushered Remy in to meet me as I sat in a chair, he decided to claim me, jumping onto my lap and pressing his little white paws against my chest.

I was his! Upon inquiring of Mary if Remy did this to everyone, she replied, "Well, he tries." He was used to being rejected and, looking at him, I could understand why. One of his ears was shrunken, much smaller than the other ear, with several lumpy hematomas. The veterinarian was at a loss to explain how this happened—perhaps a dog had chewed his ear in a vicious fight. The remaining ear was much larger, and it had been ear-nipped – crudely chopped off at the tip when Remy had been neutered after his tumultuous ride on the crowded trip to the Bronx. (This ear-nipping is a sign that a feral cat has been neutered or spayed.) To top it all off, one of his eyes was very "weepy," just as one of my eyes was. Was it the "Law of Attraction" at work?

Saying he would never win in a cat show was an understatement. If not unsightly it was even comical. I shuddered to think of this poor cat being shoved off someone's lap or even laughed at right in his face, I knew well the cruelty, and I could relate well to Remy's plight. Although I never had my ears nipped, as a child I had "ptosis of the eyelid," in which the muscle of one eyelid was so relaxed that my eyelid was always closed. In Kindergarten when I would attempt to speak with another child, he or she would not respond. They would only stare, then burst out laughing right in my face. I had to wait until I was seven years old to have this surgically corrected. You can imagine how, by this time, the damage had been done and I had retreated into my reclusive shell. It was easy to commiserate.

Arrangements were made to adopt Remy. I only wish I could have explained to him that I was coming back for him, as he slowly sauntered away from me, imagining that this was just another rejection. He turned his head to look at me one last time, a heaviness in his steps betraying his deep depression. Better times are coming, Remy – you'll see!

Remy & Mid-Night ~ Together ~ at last!

REMY & MID-NIGHT
DBA "ROMEO AND JULIET"

On a more positive note, Remy did have one admirer—a younger and decidedly most feminine velvety black cat named Mid-night, who also had been ear-nipped and released. Since they had feline aids, Mary kept them in a room apart from the other cats she was trying to adopt out. Upon suddenly opening the door of that room, it was quite humorous to see their expressions of wide-eyed surprise, as they were discovered entwined together in their cat-bed. It was soon evident that they were inseparable.

"Remy"

Out for a morning stroll

Remy was now "vet-ready" to come home with me. Mary told me that "Mid-night would be lost without Remy," and as I could not bear to separate the two lovers, I agreed to adopt Mid-night also as soon as she was cleared by the veterinarian. Mid-night had had surgery and her underside was stitched together. It was surmised that she had been surprised by a human as she was eating outdoors and, in her haste to escape, got caught on the top wires of a barbed wire fence.

Mid-night also had problems finding an adoptive pet-parent. Prior to my agreement to adopt her, Mary and her husband planned to bring her to a cat sanctuary down the shore, a good two or three hour drive. Then they would have their wedding anniversary dinner at a fine restaurant nearby. Well, as fate would have it, the sanctuary was in a deplorable condition, filthy with flies swarming around and Mary could not in good conscience leave Mid-night there. So they never had their anniversary dinner. With Mid-night in the car, they turned around and drove all the way back home. What a way to spend one's wedding anniversary – for the love of cats! But it was for the best because if this had not occurred Mid-night and Remy would have never have been together. It was fate!

I joke with Mary, that someday when she dies there will be a multitude of cats waiting to greet her at the "Rainbow Bridge."

"Mid-Night" In a "sulky" mood.

REMY'S "HOME SWEET HOME"

On March 17th, Saint Patrick's Day, Remy's kinder, gentler life in the country began — far away from the harsh rigors of the city's Market Street. Understandably, Remy had issues with rejection and food insecurity. He would ravenously gulp down his food in seeming anticipation of aggressive competition from other famished cats. And although Mary had provided all of his physical necessities, she had so many "fur children" to care for, that she was simply unable to give Remy all of the nurturing his little spirit craved.

We had no knowledge of his background, but it was apparent that he had been severely traumatized in some way. I noticed that he would duck his little head in anticipation of being struck if I approached him from above to pet him. This caused me to wonder if he had been abused in the past. I did my best to reassure him and provide a secure, protective and loving environment where he could thrive — lots of cuddles and petting, of which he never seemed to tire. It was a healing balm for my own spirit as well.

"Wherever a cat sits, there shall happiness be found."

- Stanley Spencer (1891-1959)

Before Remy came to live with me, Mary had perceived: "He knows he has no lasting place here." It took a full month of tender care and nurturing (and gourmet cat food served with regularity) before Remy began to shed his depression. Soon there was a spring in his steps instead of the customary heaviness. It seemed to me that the realization that he finally had a secure, permanent dwelling place had set in.

I was awestruck as, on one enchanted spring day, he glanced about his new woodsy surroundings, and then impulsively sprung a few feet up a tree before joyfully leaping onto the ground below. Remy was home!

I AM "THE AMAZING ANNIE"
– TO MY CAT!

After a short time had passed, Remy had stopped defensively ducking his little head when I stooped to pet him. And when I cradled him in my arms it jolted me to see his look of admiration as he unreservedly "let go" in total abandonment on my lap (right on top of my pile of bills and correspondence). Startled and pondering if this was only my imagination – it had to be, I glanced away from Remy's adoring gaze and then back again, that look was still there. My goodness, it seemed something akin to idolatry!

I pondered whether I was worthy of so much trust, then after some reflection decided that, indeed, I was. So if I, a mere mortal, could be trusted so unconditionally, why then couldn't I trust the Divine for my own needs and concerns?

"Look at the birds of the air, for they do not sow, nor do they reap, nor gather into barns. Yet your heavenly Father feeds them. Are you not much better than they?"

"Therefore, take no thought, saying, 'What shall we eat?' or 'What shall we drink?' or 'What shall we wear?' (For the Gentiles seek after all these things.) For your heavenly Father knows that you have need of all these things. But seek first the kingdom of God and His righteousness, and all these things shall be given to you."

-Matthew 6:26,31-33.

"Animals are such agreeable friends- They ask no questions; they pass no criticisms."

-George Eliot

"If man could be crossed with a cat, it would improve man but deteriorate the cat."

-Mark Twain

Resolution: I want to become the person my cat thinks I am.

Remy in a pensive mood.

"Remy"

So happy Annie's home!

KINDRED SPIRITS

Remy and I were kindred spirits. One of my most memorable experiences was during one winter when I arrived home. Remy greeted me with much yowling at the top of his voice – one might even call it singing, as if to scold me: "Where were you? I've been waiting all day!" He wouldn't stop until I rushed over and scooped him up in my arms – I barely had time to take off my coat.

At other times, when I pulled into the driveway, a friend would let Remy out of the cottage, so that he could run down the path to greet me-and what a joyful reunion it was! He wasn't miffed as Toby had been, when I would return after a long absence. I don't think Remy had an ounce of pride-he was simply so excited that I was home!

Because of his colorful personality (Mary had nicknamed him "Mr. Personality") I considered renaming him *Creamsicle*. It would have been a perfect fit, considering his orange coat and white bobby-sock paws. But I had read that a pet should only have a one or two syllable name for the sake of simplicity. Besides, Remy had been through so many changes, and he was accustomed to his name by now –but I thought it was a clever idea.

So passed the days joyfully. Remy loved to stretch out on my deck like a "cat-centerfold," as someone coined the term, sunning himself. And when I'd sit on my deck to go through my mail, he'd jump right on top of my lap, having no regard for my bills going out on time. Most nights we slept together, his soft white bobby-sock paws claiming me as he did on our first encounter at Mary's house. Like Toby, he helped me to see things in perspective, what was really important in life, as we stopped to smell the roses together. After all, what was the rush? In some ways, Remy was a teacher.

"But ask now the beasts, and they shall teach thee; and the fowls of the air, and they shall tell thee: Or speak to the earth, and it shall teach thee: and the fishes of the sea shall declare onto thee."

-Job 12:7-8

The author as a child on grandma's farm in communion with calf.

A RAUCOUS REUNION

After about two and a half months had passed, Mary said that Mid-night had completed her veterinary care and was ready to rejoin her partner. Mid-night was nowhere as docile as Remy – she was more like the cat "with all the affection of a dead houseplant" I told you earlier. Remy was fire and Mid-night was ice as far as our relationship was concerned. Of course, we had not an inkling of what her previous experiences with humans had been like.

Mary told me, from her vast experiences in dealing with cats of various temperaments, that she felt Mid-night would take several years to become socialized. I found this difficult to believe because of my very successful dealings with Toby and Remy. As it turned out, however, Mary was absolutely right.

Remy in an after-dinner nap.

"Mid-Night"

Mid-night was a wild one. It had taken Mary and her daughter all the strength they could muster just to wrestle Mid-night into the cage to bring her to the vet. It was no wonder that no one would adopt her! Mid-night was her own worst enemy. Cold and indifferent, she rebuffed all of my attempts at friendship. The main reason I adopted her was because Remy loved her. So now Remy had the role as my main comforter, with Mid-night as what I called the "auxiliary cat." I hoped things would improve in time, but for a while it seemed hopeless. Amazingly, Mid-night would finally succumb to my effort several years later just as Mary had predicted, but more about that later.

For the present, my main objective was to unite the two lovers who were so intimate just two and a half months ago. Since they were so well acquainted, I deemed it unnecessary to introduce them slowly, as I had read one should do with two cats who never met. Boy, I couldn't have been more wrong!

To my chagrin, when I released Mid-night from her cage to be reunited with Remy, there was a LOT of hissing, as if they had never met! I assumed that it would be a very happy occasion but it was the opposite. It was very upsetting and even very frightening to watch. I guess Remy had claimed his paradise on earth and considered Mid-night an intruder. Later Mary told me that, to a cat, two and a half months was a long time. I only wish I had known that sooner.

To my great relief, it didn't take long before the two were in loving sync again. Unlike humans, Mid-night was oblivious to Remy's flaws as she gazed at her "older man" adoringly.

Remy on the other hand, gave me the impression of taking her affections for granted, even being aloof at times—a mite chauvinistic I thought. But then they would take up where they left off before their separation. Their romance resumed... Remy having a far-away look in his eyes, perhaps reminiscing about something that had transpired before that fateful trip to the Bronx....

Remy was not so chivalrous, however, at dinnertime. One could say that his manners were atrocious. Although the two had separate bowls, as Remy ate from his bowl he would continuously glance to the side of Mid-night's dish as she ate. He would ravenously consume his own food before hastily running over to gluttonously devour every last morsel on Mid-night's dish. This, in spite of the fact that he had had most of his teeth extracted by the veterinarian before his adoption. It didn't deter him in the least. He would then promptly throw up from all this rushing to eat. The solution was simple. Just separating them at dinner did the trick.

Remy got a real kick out of playing a game with Mid-night. He would hide, stealthily crouching on the side of my deck in anticipation of Mid-night as she would unassumingly pass by, unaware of any intended foul play. At this point Remy would suddenly run and playfully pounce on her, reveling in her startled reaction as she was caught off-guard.

"We have three cats. It's like having children, but there is no tuition involved."

-Ron Reagan

"Way down deep, we're all motivated by the same urges. Cats have the courage to live by them."

-Jim Davis

REMY DBA "COMFORT CAT"

Soon Remy was to play a new, unexpected role in my life. During a routine doctor visit I was informed, to my horror, that I might need open-heart surgery. A subsequent echocardiogram confirmed it. It would require several months of recovery time, during which I would be unable to work. To say I was in shock was an understatement. How in the world would I manage? Having little else but God on my side, I went into surgery which was, thankfully, successful. A friend stayed with my two "fur-children" 24/7 and saw to all their needs.

After fifteen days of recovery, and terribly missing my two cats, I was able to return home. What a joyful reunion it was!

Remy, of course, was anxious to assume his usual place on me, and I had to be most careful to strategically position him after this surgery. His vibrant purring seemed to penetrate deeply within me, not only physically but as a pervading peace. I have no doubt he helped speed up my healing. Mid-night, on the other hand, was as usual, a kitty to be reckoned with as she resumed her "cool kitty" act. But at least she was a loving companion to Remy while I was away, which was no small consolation.

While recovering, I watched a lot of DVDs. Remy was fascinated by a certain DVD which displayed nature scenes and a variety of birds. When the birds came onto the screen, he would stealthily creep up to the flat screen and place his paw over the bird, then with a puzzled look walk away, when he was unable to catch his prey. Although it was most comical to watch, I also felt somewhat sorry to see his disappointment!

Mama Cat's Visitation

It had been about three years since Remy came to live with me, when we had an unexpected visitor. I had just gotten out of my car and was running toward the house, when a large, orange shorthair cat appeared in the middle of the driveway. Struggling to maintain my balance as I tried to avoid tripping over her, I nearly fell over. The cat then disappeared and I was left alone standing in the driveway. This cat was substantially larger than Remy, with the same orange colored coat, but lacking his bobby-sock white paws.

Incredulous, I called my friend, Interfaith Minister Maria D'Andrea, who revealed to me that it had been Remy's mother from the Spirit World, and that she was very protective of her little boy. I dreaded the thought that this could be a sign that my Remy would soon be departing from this world. I tried not to think about it.

No one knew for sure how old Remy had been when I adopted him, but he had been substantially older than Mid-night. He was now showing signs of aging, as he gradually grew more feeble. Soon his time came to be reunited with his devoted mother-just one year after her "visitation."

Remy did have one fault that I permitted him to indulge in. He had a double-wide cat scratcher, which for some reason known only to himself, he refused to use. Instead, he would feverishly scratch the door frame of my front door and the post near the entrance of the stairs leading to the deck. However, he never did any harm to any of the furniture in the house, for which I was thankful. He seemed to enjoy this so intensely, standing on his two hind legs, arching his back as he scratched, that I didn't have the heart to stop it.

Since I had no one else to answer to about my house, I felt this was my own business. (I know that there are some who would be horrified at this.) Now, I tenderly fingered the deep grooves in the wood, as they brought back a flood of memories, vowing never to paint over it as long as I owned the house. Remy had made his marks and I simply refused to cover them up, crazy as that may seem. In light of his other virtues and the joy he had brought me, this was a very small price to pay.

"Remy"

"Sleep in Heavenly Peace."

"Dustin"

Two weeks after Remy's passing I was taking a walk down a dusty country road as I reminisced, when I came across a coal-black butterfly with bright blue dots bordering it's wings, just lying in the middle of the road. Wondering what I should do, as I was hesitant to pick it up, since it could be injured. I didn't want to make matters worse. The butterfly suddenly rose up and flew in a circle around me several times at my waist's height before following me for some time, as I walked down the road.

I thought of calling my cat-rescuer friend, Mary, to tell her, but had my doubts if I should, since she had sometimes dismissed my "tall tales," telling me that I had a very vivid imagination. But when I decided to take a chance anyway, to my amazement she didn't seem the least bit surprised.

She related to me that she never knew that there was such a thing as a black butterfly, but that she had also seen one around the time of Remy's death, with colorful dots bordering its wings! This only helped to validate my experience.

Soon afterwards I went shopping and came across a granite statue of a cross with the word "HOPE" written across the bottom and a black butterfly with bright blue dots bordering its wings in the center of the cross. Of course, I promptly purchased it, and placed it on a shelf in my bedroom where I could always view it. A lovely momento.

Another encounter with butterflies that a friend and myself witnessed was when an orange (Remy's color) butterfly stubbornly kept making attempts at getting into my cottage through the closed front door. My friend kept exclaiming, "That butterfly was trying to get in!" over and over.

REMY'S RETURN

Remy made his presence known one day to us. As we sat on my sofa we suddenly felt his little paws walking over us, very similar to my experience with Toby. Remy also feverishly kneaded me, as he often did in the past. Welcome back!

From time to time, as I lay in bed, I would feel something that felt just like a cat jumping on my bed, then little paw-print indentations on my blanket. Since this was invisible, I could not be sure whether they were from Remy or Toby, but I believe they both come to say "hello" now and then.

An elderly neighbor named Carol and I were sitting outdoors talking, when she exclaimed that she saw the shadow of a cat run by me. When I turned to look I saw nothing there. Carol knew nothing of my ghostly visitations.

Another neighbor and I both saw an orange cat in the woods by her house, which then disappeared. She kept exclaiming over and over: "I saw that cat—it was there!"

I was surprised to find that these apparitions are not uncommon when I researched: www.ghostcats.com on the computer.

You'll be amazed what you'll find there.

A "MID-NIGHT MIRACLE"

Mid-night, now bereft of her lover, was refusing food, eating only paltry amounts for about a week. Her depression was of great concern to me, as she mourned her great loss-my heart ached for her. But to my relief she soon began eating normally. Previously a "kitty to be reckoned with," she had rebuffed all of my attempts at a relationship. Rudyard Kipling must have had a Mid-night in his life when he penned: "I am the cat who walks by himself."

And as Rod McKuen observed:

> *"Cats have it all-admiration, an endless sleep, and company only when they want it."*

That fit Mid-night to a "tee!" I might add gourmet cat food to the list. Perhaps I shouldn't have been so surprised when Mid-night abruptly approached me, since I really did pray for a "Mid-night Miracle." But I couldn't help being astonished at this unusual turn of events.

I ran down a checklist of her needs:

1. Food in her dish? Check.
2. Water? Check.
3. Clean litter box? Check.

What in the world could she want? "I think she wants to be petted," my friend commented. It just couldn't be, I thought, after over four years. Mary had been right after all.

Tentatively, I reached out my hand to pet her–and she accepted!

I guess Mid-night thought I would just have to do, now that her Prince Charming was no longer available. Of course, I could never take the place of another cat, particularly one of Remy's caliber, but I was better than nothing, right? A cat has to be practical, after all. I wondered about the thought processes in her kitty-mind that caused this change of heart. Was it love, convenience, or simply survival? I preferred to think that LOVE WON!

Mid-night, to my amazement and relief, adjusted quite well to her "new normal" after this traumatic event, and life went on. I only wish I could recover so quickly-life would be so much simpler (and my therapist would be out of business).

It took some time to get over the shock of the formerly aloof and elusive Mid-night, now coming to me for affection, as she displayed a new vulnerability I had never seen before. She took Remy's place in bed at night with me, as she curled up with her tail wrapped around herself, softly purring. And her sad green eyes would follow me as I headed to my car to go for a drive and light up again upon my return.

I sometimes wondered if Mid-night saw any ghostly apparitions of Toby and Remy as I had. Probably, since cats don't have the biases that most humans have about such phenomena, being more sensitive and open. They were never brainwashed as humans are in childhood and told: "There are no such things as ghosts." To a cat, seeing into another spiritual dimension is simply a part of life—no big deal!

A donkey saw into the spiritual realm in Numbers 22:27-28 of the Old Testament, which her human owner at first could not see:

"When the donkey saw the angel of the Lord, she fell down under Balaam, and the anger of Balaam was inflamed, and he struck the donkey with a staff. Then the Lord opened the mouth of the donkey, and she said to Balaam, "What have I done to you, that you have struck me these three times?"

Later on the Lord opened up the eyes of the man so that he could see the angel.

So this makes me believe that there may have been times that Mid-night could have seen ghostly apparitions that I could not. I only wish that Mid-night could talk to me like the donkey did and tell me. (For those who are interested, read the rest of the chapter to find out what the angel said about striking the donkey.)

"Mid-night"

"The hardest thing of all is to find a black cat in a dark room, especially if there is no cat."

-Confucius

IN CLOSING...

It's just over two years since Remy's passing, and Midnight is still with me. Although she is in good health, she is getting on in years and there is a certain fragility about her, with her velvety black fur now sprinkled with gray. I cherish each day with her and hope that she will remain with me for a long time to come. Although I must get on with my life, I often reminisce about my other fur-children, Toby and Remy, whom I know are expectantly waiting to be reunited with me someday across the Rainbow Bridge. What a wonderful day that will be! Until that time, photographs and fond memories will have to see me through.

It is my heartfelt desire that this book will help to encourage the adoption of older cats, even those with problems. Although Remy's physical flaws were, frankly, a bit hard to get used to, I focused on his awesome eyes, mesmerized. And I preferred my feral cats, Toby, Remy and Mid-night, over the most expensive pedigrees. They brought me such joy!

Like a fully matured rose whose petals reach out, the mature, emotionally seasoned cat provides warmth and comfort, thus making an excellent companion. And particularly for older people, they are not as frisky as kittens. They are not as hard to keep up with.

My prayer is that you will give such cats a chance.

Thank you, and God Bless.

The Author

APPENDIX

CATS AND COMPUTERS

Cats don't like them. Mid-night told me so, confiding in me that she is in complete agreement with Dr. Andrew Weil, who discourages the overuse of technology by humans. It is simply not the way we are made, and we should be doing more things like taking long walks in nature. And according to Mid-night, this includes lavishing her with a lot of petting and special care <u>because she says that she's a part of nature</u> – a very convincing argument from a very smart cat who knows how to get what she wants! I must say, a very clever feline.

My own take is that the more the human senses are involved in communicating, the more satisfying, fulfilling, and intimate those relationships will be. Case in point: When talking on the phone, we are deprived of the senses of sight, smell and touch.

Only hearing is experienced (although one can sense inflections and moods from someone's voice). There is even more sensory deprivation from texting, where no senses are involved, not even hearing. Ditto for a cold email on the computer.

Of course, phones and computers are necessary, but at the same time one must recognize that our senses play a major role in what makes us fully human. We should do our best to utilize them if we wish to have more enriching relationships. Mid-night says that cats are more in tune with their own nature than humans are. Ouch!

So an important element is that, due to their availability which we unfortunately often lack from our busy family and friends, our cats and other pets provide much needed psychological and even physical benefits.

When a ten-year study was conducted by the Stroke Center at the University of Minnesota, cat owners were discovered to possess a 30% less risk of heart attacks! (*Cat Fancy magazine*, Jan. 2010).

Also, Johannes Odendaal, author of *Pets & Our Mental Health*, conducted an experiment which measured changes in brain chemistry between dogs and their owners while petting, etc. (Vantage Press, 2002). Increases during these interactions with dogs include: Dopamine, which is known to create pleasurable experiences and Beta-phenylethylamine, which decreases fatigue and promotes a positive mood.

Cortisol was discovered to decrease with positive interaction between dogs and owners, such as petting.

Prior to his death, Johannes Odendaal was being interviewed, and when asked if petting a cat would yield the same results, his answer was a resounding "yes."

Of course, there are many more examples to scientifically back up the physical and mental benefits of the pet-human relationship which are not within the scope of this book. New discoveries are always being made.

Hint: My elderly aunt in Nevada, who wishes to remain anonymous, tells me that her landlord actually charges $20.00 more rent if a tenant has a pet. When her doctor wrote a note to her landlord that having her little dog helped her blood pressure, the landlord waived the extra $20.00. Hey, it's worth a try!

Ms. Kitty Kat
P.O. Box 923
Gouldsboro, PA. 18424

101

DATE MAY 6, 2019

PAY TO THE ORDER OF GREEDY LANDLORD $ 20.⁰⁰/₁₀₀

TWENTY AND ⁰⁰/₁₀₀ ———————— DOLLARS

MEMO RENT   Ms. Kitty Kat

LOOK FOR FRAUD-DETERRING FEATURES INCLUDING THE SECURITY WEAVE AND HEAT-REACTIVE INK. DETAILS ON BACK.

NOTES

Made in the USA
Middletown, DE
20 December 2020